Pits and Looms

A photographic look at some of Lancashire's traditional industries

Text by Peter Riley

P & D Riley

First published 2003

P & D Riley
12 Bridgeway East
Cheshire WA7 6LD
England

E-mail: pdriley@ntlworld.com

ISBN: 1 874712 64 6

British Library Cataloguing in Publication Data
A catalogue record for this book is available from the British Library

Printed in England.

Introduction

Lancashire, the heart of British industrial might for a century and a half, was home to hundreds of coal mines and textile mills. These two major industries contributed to the growth of the once mighty British Empire, made major inroads into providing a chunk of cash to the American economy during the 19th century, and saw the tiny British Isles emerge as the most powerful and richest country on earth.

The coal mining industry provided employment for millions, either directly through the pits or through such spin-off companies as coal merchants, while the mills provided steady if sometimes dangerous work for tens of thousands of men, women and children, whose products were the envy of the world.

In this book we take a look at both these industrial giants in their hey-day through a unique and fascinating collection of photographs showing the depth and intricacies of the work involved throughout the past century in getting the coal from the coal face to the customer, and getting raw cotton to the mills and outputting it in the shape of garments.

They worked hard in the pits and at the loom and none more than the lads and lasses of Lancashire, to whom this book is a tribute. Unfortunately the trades and skills of Lancashire were soon copied by other nations around the world, notably the Far East, which subsequently saw British industry decline.

Peter Riley

Peter Riley is the author and editor of numerous local history titles, including *Wythenshawe A Bygone Era* (with Susan Hall) ; *Wythenshawe Hall and the Tatton family ; Heaton Hall and the Egerton Family ; A History of Peel Hall* (with Susan Hall) ; *A Short History of Culcheth* (with Oscar Plant) ; *The Highways and Byways of Jack the Ripper ; Place to Place ; Stockton Heath A Bygone Era ; Culcheth A Bygone Era ; Lowton A Bygone Era ; Knutsford A Bygone Era ; Bury A Bygone Era ; Leigh, Tyldesley and Atherton A Bygone Era ; Newton-le-Willows A Bygone Era; Hyde A Bygone Era ; Newton-le-Willows in Bygone Days ; A History of Leigh ; A History of Atherton ; A History of Tyldesley ; A History of Astley ; A History of Bolton ; A History of Widnes ; A History of Flixton; Then and Now (Leigh); Warrington Then and Now ; Manchester Then and Now.*

Acknowledgements

The publisher would like to thank the following for their help during
the preparation of this book

The Local Studies Unit, Manchester Central Library
Wigan Metropolitan Borough Council
Leigh Library
Salford Local History Library
Christine Baylie of Lewis Textile Museum, Blackburn

EoH

Coal Mining in Lancashire, 1936. This was once one of the most common sights in the industrial North of England, with men arriving or leaving work on bicycles. There was a special camaraderie among miners and their families, and it is little wonder that this part of Britain was known as the workshop of the world. Coal and other fuels were produced by tough, no-nonsense men who relied exclusively on the local pit for their livelihood. When pits were the scene of accidents or deaths, the whole community were intimately involved, and when they closed for one reason or another it was often the death knell for whole towns. When this picture was taken, however, British coal was at its zenith and the future looked rosy – if dirty!

Preparing to go down the pit: There was always a look of apprehension on the faces of miners preparing to drop a mile underground, where they would remain for the next eight to ten hours. The days work would not begin at the bottom of the shaft, for these men would often have to walk or crawl to the pit face which could be two miles away. To say it was a tough life is an understatement!

At the coal face: Crawling on all fours, squatting in unimaginable confined spaces was often the lot of pit men, particularly in the 1930s before modern technology was introduced in the pits. In pre– nationalisation days the private companies who owned them would often refuse to invest in machinery that would have made the lot of miners a whole lot easier. Not that mining is easy for anyone, but just watching these men at work is enough to make us all appreciate just what a brilliant job they did to keep our homes and factories working.

At the sidings: Tons of coal and other fuels were regularly kept in trucks in railway sidings alongside the colliery, usually waiting to be shipped to power stations or coal merchants across Lancashire or other parts of the country. It is a sight that, alas, is no longer seen in this part of the country.

Loading coal at the washery in 1936:
Despite the hardship of the miners digging out the coal, Lancashire housewives even in the 1930s were a fussy lot and did not like receiving coal with dust on it. This meant the pits normally washed the fuel before shipping it out.

Sizing Coal, 1936:

Another important job in the collieries was sizing the different types of coal, for many housewives would not buy tiny lumps, while others preferred the larger nuts. This meant an extra job for many local people as sizing coal was a time consuming task, but one pits thought necessary to keep their customers happy. It was also a useful way for spotting and discarding lumps of coal which, because of the content of some metallic substance, would not burn well – another definite point of issue with Lancashire folk who would think nothing of changing their regular coal merchant if he did not supply "proper" coal.

Second screening and sizing of coal:
Impurities could often sneak into coal stocks despite the manual process, so a second screening and sizing was carried out to ensure that coal merchants only received the highest standards of fuel available.

Separating washed coal 1936

Washing coal 1936:

The idea of washing coal may seem a humorous thing to do considering the colour of coal, but the idea was certainly sane as far as pit bosses were concerned, particularly in the days of private pits before nationalisation. The gravity of coal is so low that it almost floats on water, while rock, which can not always be spotted in the dust, always sinks as it is much heavier. Thus all the small pieces of coal that would not be economical for hand washing and screening was put in machines that would separate the coal from the dirt and the floating coal, often referred to as 'diamonds', would be poured into sieves.

The Conveyor Belt

Coal from the pit brow to the railway trucks had to travel along a conveyor belt as part of the journey prior to being dropped into mechanical riddles where it was sorted and screened before being shot into a chute where it was dropped into railway trucks. At each stage sharp eyed women, lads and drivers would be on the lookout for impurities.

Screens in Wigan in 1910

Drawing coal at a Bacup pit
This photograph gives us a good example of just how tight space was in most of Lancashire's pits, and pushing a truck would take considerable strength. No room for large machinery here!

Inside Victoria Pit, Wigan
A fascinating study of life at the bottom of a pit shaft where shoring walls was obviously a vital job.

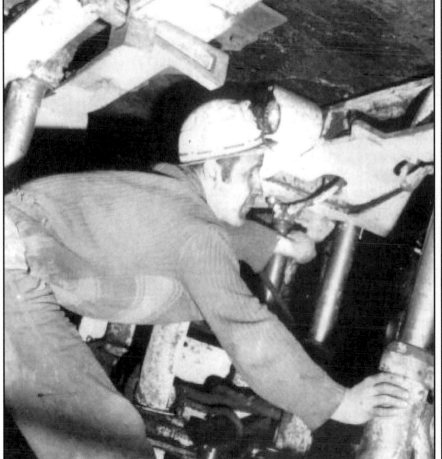

Agecroft Colliery:

By means of hydraulic rams these miners (top) at Agecroft Colliery in Salford in the 1960s were able to install powerful chocks to support the roof at the coal face. A pressure of about 200 tons was exerted on the roof.

Once into position at the coal face it took the effort of one man to adjust the pressure by means of hydraulic valves. This was an important feature in modern mining, making the coal face much safer.

Queuing for wages

This is a fascinating photograph that was taken at Brackley Colliery near Bolton in December 1939. The men, dressed in typical Lancashire garb of raincoat, flat cap and neck scarf, were lining up to collect their wages for Christmas which was only a few days away. For many pit workers the Christmas holiday was the only time they saw daylight during the winter.

Peel Hill Pit, Salford.

When this picture was taken in 1910 the streets of Walkden were a common route for these horse and carts carrying coal from Peel Hill Colliery. The pit's owners would sell fuel directly to their customers and these powerful but gentle beasts were a popular sight in the district.

The Dive Underground in Atherton:
This photograph was taken at the old Fletcher Burrows Colliery in Atherton near Leigh, and shows pitmen getting ready for going underground. One visitor to the pit early in the 20th century wrote: "The change from daylight to darkness is dramatic in its suddenness. The whole drop is 600 yards, or four times the height of St Paul's Cathedral in London….The air presses on the drums of the ears; there is a catch of the breath; the stomach is left at the pit head, and overtakes the toner later; there is a feeling of utter helplessness…"

Recovering bodies at Salford:
What every pit family dreaded! A pit disaster affected the whole community and everyone would turn up at the pit waiting for news of those who had suffered, always asking the question "Do we know if anyone was killed?" And then the long wait for news. This photograph showed a group waiting to recover bodies after tragic explosion at Clifton Hall Colliery in 1885 which claimed 178 lives.

Pemberton Colliery, 1900:
Pit ponies continued to be used in some mines until the 20th century, and here we see two of them being trained above ground for the tough job soon to follow.

Flue Scrapers, Salford:

Flue scraping must have been one of the filthiest and most unpleasant jobs in a colliery, and these men, one in clogs and the other in boots, were responsible for scraping dirt and soot from inside boilers and flues. This photograph dates from the early 20th century and was taken at Newtown Colliery, Salford, which closed in 1961.

Mine Working in 1878:
This sketch speaks for itself, showing as it does the appalling conditions in Lancashire's mines in the 19th century when Britain prided itself on being the most forward looking nation on earth!

Parsonage Pit, Leigh:
This pit closed in the early 1990s and on the site now stands a modern but uninspiring shopping centre. This was one of the town's major pits, close to the town centre, and its closure caused much distress and unemployment in Leigh.

Colliers Strike, 1912
Strikes among miners were becoming more common in the early 20th century than they had been in the Victorian era, as colliers realised they had the right to better pay and conditions, but most strikes brought extreme hardship to families. In 1912 soup kitchens were set up throughout Lancashire to help feed the families of striking pitmen, and a fuel shortage meant sneaking onto coal heaps and picking whatever bits of coal or coke was available, though anyone caught could face a jail sentence.

Bickershaw Colliery, Leigh:

Another victim of the massive pit closures of the early 1990, Bickershaw was connected underground to nearby Golborne pit, and the loss meant hardship to many, and a huge decline in the prosperity of both towns.

Woman Pit Worker, 1917:

The First World War saw Britain with a severe shortage of men to serve in the battlefield trenches of France, so women were enlisted to help out and work in traditional male industries. One of these, of course, was mining, and this magnificent photograph shows better than any words just how hard the work was. The size of the bag of coal on this woman's bag was huge, and it depicts perfectly just how capable women were at doing any type of job in the fight to keep Britain moving.

Cotton Picking in the 1930s:
In the 1930's picking cotton in America's deep south was as backbreaking and time consuming as it had ever been in the days of slavery, but mechanisation did not come into effect until after the Second World War so it was a necessary if unpleasant chore to get the raw material for Lancashire's mills.

Unloading Cotton at Manchester Docks:
Manchester Docks was once one of the major ports in England, and millions of tons of cotton were imported here to be shipped to Lancashire mill towns, such as Oldham, Leigh and Burnley.

Checking American Cotton:
Quality has always been paramount to Lancashire's cotton industry, and this photograph shows a large bale being checked.

Setting up cotton for inspection:
With buyers travelling from throughout almost every town in Lancashire to buy cotton in huge quantities, it was imperative they could easily check what they were paying for, and this warehouse in Manchester was geared up to cope with the expected rush to buy new imports.

Sampling cotton:

Cotton proud! That was the boast of Lancashire's mills and they were very fussy about what they paid good money for, which meant that their representatives or buyers would not hesitate to get down on hands and knees in a warehouse to take a keen look at the quality. This picture shows one such inspection of a cotton sample at Manchester in the 1920s.

Storage of cotton in Trafford Park:

Inspections were one thing, but finding room for the huge imports were another for the British firms responsible for bringing the goods into the country, and this photograph gives us a good idea of the size of a warehouse in Trafford Park, Manchester's major industrial area, which was used for storage of cotton prior to it being transported across the county and beyond.

Weighing American Cotton:
Getting value for money is always an essential part of any transaction, and in Lancashire in its cotton hey-day the weight firms paid for was the weight they expected, so this scale was used daily to make sure. And to be doubly certain there was an overseer on hand to check there was no cheating going on!

Steam train in Manchester Docks:
Well into the 1950s Trafford Park and Manchester Docks were linked by an extensive railway network which meant goods could arrive in the country and once checked by customs, inspected by buyers and bought, could then be easily moved from docks to warehouse or beyond in the quickest time possible. No need for huge lorries and congested motorways in those days. The train took the strain!

A Lancashire spinning mill:
In the 19th century Lancashire saw mills spring up quicker than daffodils in spring, and they were massive constructions, designed to impress as much as to be practical. Until as recently as the 1960s there were hundreds of these buildings across Lancashire, and although the majority of them have since been demolished, some remain and have been converted into smaller industrial units. But they remain as a reminder to the county's former industrial might.

Breaking open a bale:
The moment of truth! An air of expectation at the mill as the first bale of a new batch is opened ready to start its long journey from raw cotton to new clothing.

Beginning the mixing process:
The United States and Egypt were the main source of supply for wool entering Britain, with the rest of the British Empire being mainly responsible for cotton imports. These all headed to Lancashire where they were processed into cloth and then exported again!

A scutching machine:
This was the process where cotton was opened mechanically and cleaned before being formed into a continuous Lap.

A Carding Machine:
Looking like an old fashioned printing press, the carding machine worked on fibres that had been partially straightened and cleaned before spinning. The yarn processed through a Carding Machine was generally coarser than combed yarn.

Combing the cotton:
This method was necessary to eliminate any foreign matter or short fibres, leaving longer ones that were easier to straighten and spin.

Above:
The Drawing Process where the threads of a warp were drawn through the eyes of a Heald.

Left: Slubbing:
This was the name given to relatively thick strands of fibre.

Intermediate:

Part way through the process of fabric making, the machinery needed constant attention to ensure that the cotton was being processed correctly.

Left:
Roving Frames
Relatively fine strands of fibre, known as a Roving, used in the final or later process of preparing the cotton for spinning were placed on these large but delicate machines.

Below:
Spinning Mule
The Mule drew out cotton fibres by combing and were generally operated by a spinner and two piecers. The Spinning Mule was regarded as inferior to the later ring spindle which was popular in the USA and which could operate at a faster rate.

Right: Ring Frame

This was a yarn spinning method in which a thin strand of fibre, with very little twist, was fed to a rotating ring feature known as a traveller. Inside the ring was a fast rotating bobbin that accepted the yarn.

Left:
Making the Warp
Being a number of threads in long lengths running parallel which were used for weaving.

Top:
Warpers Beam:

Left:
Inserting a Cop of yarn
A form of yarn package spun on a mule spindle.

Warp entering the Healds: between two beams about five feet apart; half way between the beams the warp passed through a frame work of looped threads, called healds.

Cotton fabric from the loom:

Finishing Machine:

The Finishing Machine, looking like a gigantic waterwheel, was responsible for putting the final processes onto yarn, such as smoothness, drape and lustre.

Ring Frame Assembly:

Building Ring Frames was an important part of allowing increased production in British mills, for ring spinning gave mill owners the chance to make even larger profits, for these innovative machines allowed unskilled workers to watch them. Unlike the more traditional mule, that had been the backbone of Lancashire's mills and demanded skilled spinners, the Ring Frame spun continuously and was worked by employees who earned far less.